21ST CENTURY DEBATES

TERRORISM
THE IMPACT ON OUR LIVES

ALEX WOOLF

HODDER
Wayland

an imprint of Hodder Children's Books

21st Century Debates Series

Genetics • Surveillance • Internet • Media • Artificial Intelligence • Climate Change • Energy • Rainforests • Waste, Recycling and Reuse • Endangered Species • Air Pollution • An Overcrowded World? • Food Supply • Water Supply • World Health • Global Debt • The Drugs Trade • New Religious Movements • Racism • Violence in Society

Produced for Hodder Wayland by White-Thomson Publishing Ltd, 2/3 St Andrew's Place, Lewes, East Sussex BN7 1UP

© 2003 White-Thomson Publishing Ltd

Published in Great Britain in 2003 by Hodder Wayland, an imprint of Hodder Children's Books.

Project editor: Kelly Davis
Commissioning editor: Steve White-Thomson
Proofreader: David C. Sills, Proof Positive Reading Service
Series design: Chris Halls, Mind's Eye Design, Lewes
Book design: Malcolm Walker
Picture research: Shelley Noronha, Glass Onion Pictures

British Library Cataloguing in Publication Data
Woolf, Alex
   Terrorism. - (21st Century Debates)
   1. Terrorism - Juvenile literature
   I. Title II. 303.6'25
ISBN: 0 7502 4068 7

Printed and bound in Hong Kong
Hodder Children's Books, a division of Hodder Headline Ltd, 338 Euston Road, London NW1 3BH

Picture acknowledgements: Camera Press 35 (Fred David); Corbis 44; Howard Davies/Exile Images 14; Hulton Archive 9; Popperfoto 6 (Bazuki Muhammed), 12, 15 (Hurriyet), 19 (Moshin Raza), 21, 25, 27 (Jason Reed), 29, 31 (Andrea Comas), 33 (Hector Mata), 34, 36, 38, 41, 42 (Paul McErlane), 43 (Jamal Saidi), 47 (Reuters/Sean Adair), 48 (Suhaid Salem), 49, 51, 52, 53 (Win McNamee), 54 (Reuben Baxter), 58, 59, cover background (Reuters/Peter Morgan); Science Photo Library 55; Topham 4, 10, 13, 16, 17, 22, 30, 57, cover foreground.

Cover: foreground picture shows a member of the Ulster Freedom Fighters; background picture shows firemen at work near the base of the destroyed World Trade Center after 11 September 2001.

weblinks

You don't need a computer to use this book. But, for readers who do have access to the Internet, the book provides links to recommended websites which offer additional information and resources on the subject.

You will find weblinks boxes like this on some pages of the book.

weblinks

For an in-depth look at the events of September 11 go to www.waylinks.co.uk /21debatesterrorism

waylinks.co.uk

To help you find the recommended websites easily and quickly, weblinks are provided on our own website, **waylinks.co.uk.** These take you straight to the relevant websites and save you typing in the Internet address yourself.

Internet safety

↗ Never give out personal details, which include: your name, address, school, telephone number, email address, password and mobile number.

↗ Do not respond to messages which make you feel uncomfortable – tell an adult.

↗ Do not arrange to meet in person someone you have met on the Internet.

↗ Never send your picture or anything else to an online friend without a parent's or teacher's permission.

↗ If you see anything that worries you, tell an adult.

A note to adults
Internet use by children should be supervised. We recommend that you install filtering software which blocks unsuitable material.

Website content

The weblinks for this book are checked and updated regularly. However, because of the nature of the Internet, the content of a website may change at any time, or a website may close down without notice. While the Publishers regret any inconvenience this may cause readers, they cannot be responsible for the content of any website other than their own.

HODDER
Wayland

CONTENTS

WHAT IS TERRORISM?

Systematic violence or legitimate struggle?

weblinks

For more information about the motives that lie behind different definitions of terrorism go to www.waylinks.co.uk/21debatesterrorism

Terrorism can be defined as the use of violence against civilians in order to achieve political aims. Unlike other forms of protest, such as strikes and peaceful demonstrations, terrorist acts always involve violence or the threat of violence. Terrorism differs from an act of war against enemy soldiers or military targets, because its targets are non-combatants, or civilians. Finally, terrorism is different from criminal or random forms of violence because its aims are political – concerned with how a state is governed or how its people are treated.

We all have an image of what a typical terrorist looks like. But how often do we think about the motives of the man behind the mask, and what originally led him down the path of violence?

A political word

The word 'terrorism' is often used by people to make a political point, for example to condemn their enemies. It can mean different things, or refer to different activities, depending on who is using the term. A government might label a violent street protest by its political opponents as terrorism. Those same political opponents might similarly describe the government's response to their street protest – riot police, tear gas and the like – as an act of terrorism. It is therefore important when hearing the word 'terrorism' to think about the possible motives of the person who is saying it.

There is no general agreement in the world today on what terrorism actually is. For example, there are many groups in existence who do not regard themselves as terrorists, but whose actions fit the definition on page 4. These groups, and their supporters, might claim that their use of violence is 'legitimate' because it is aimed at overthrowing an unjust or repressive regime. They might call themselves freedom fighters engaged in a struggle for national liberation. Few of these people would call themselves terrorists. This has given rise to the saying, 'one man's terrorist is another man's freedom fighter'.

As this phrase implies, there are different ways of defining, and therefore judging, groups that engage in political violence. Defined by their goals (as freedom fighters), they can appear justified, even heroic. Defined by their methods (terror), they can seem like criminals and murderers. The disagreement over the meaning of terrorism reflects the wider conflict between those countries who oppose and feel threatened by terrorism, and those countries and peoples who broadly support the aims and aspirations of so-called 'terrorist' groups.

VIEWPOINTS

'We have always opposed terrorism. But terrorism is one thing and a national struggle against occupation is another. We are against terrorism.... Nevertheless, we support the struggle against occupation waged by national liberation movements.'
President Hafez el-Assad of Syria in a speech to the 21st Convention of Workers Unions in Syria, 1986

'The idea that one person's "terrorist" is another's "freedom fighter" cannot be sanctioned. Freedom fighters or revolutionaries don't blow up buses containing non-combatants; terrorist murderers do. Freedom fighters don't set out to capture and slaughter schoolchildren; terrorist murderers do.... It is a disgrace that democracies would allow the treasured word "freedom" to be associated with acts of terrorists.'
US Senator Henry Jackson, 1985, quoted in Binyamin Netanyahu. **Terrorism: How the West Can Win**

The tactics of terror

Oppressive regimes often use terror to suppress rebels at home and abroad, and to weaken the governments of rival states. However, in modern times terrorism is just as often the weapon of the weak. It is frequently used by small groups against more powerful governments. Groups who employ terrorist tactics usually lack the resources to engage the armed forces of a country in open conflict, so they operate in secret, seeking out a government's most vulnerable areas, and attacking when least expected.

Such terrorist groups have widely differing long-term aims. Some are struggling to overthrow a foreign power that is occupying their country; others wish to increase the power and influence of their own brand of religious or political extremism. Whatever their intentions, they are usually small, tight-knit groups fighting much larger forces which have greater military and economic power. For this

A vital aim of all acts of terrorism is to attract publicity to a particular cause. The 11 September attacks on the USA were reported in newspapers and on TV all around the world.

reason, virtually all terrorist groups tend to use similar tactics.

Firstly, they aim to advertise themselves and their cause. Today's media are very efficient at gathering news from distant places and transmitting it almost instantly to an international audience, and terrorists have taken full advantage of this. Bombings and assassinations grab attention and newspaper headlines. The hijacking of an airliner is full of drama and suspense, and the identity of the group responsible is usually flashed around the world on television, giving massive publicity to their cause.

Secondly, terrorists try to make the government and its supporters feel insecure and demoralized. By making their attacks in high-profile locations, such as the heart of a city's administrative or commercial centre, or by assassinating senior politicians, terrorists like to create the impression that they can strike anywhere. Their aim is to cause panic, and to gain an image of power and ruthlessness that might lead a government to surrender to their demands out of fear.

Thirdly, terrorists try to provoke the government into reacting violently. This may reduce support for the government, and generate public sympathy for the group's cause. Some terrorist groups have made this their central strategy. For instance, the Fronte de Liberation Nationale (FLN), an Algerian nationalist group opposing the French occupation of their country in the 1950s, bombed marketplaces and other crowded locations to goad the French government into violent suppression. The French reacted in just the way intended, treating all those not of European origin as terrorist suspects and thereby alienating the entire native Algerian population.

FACT

The National Liberation Army or Ejercito de Liberación National (ELN) of Colombia is an example of a terrorist group that tries to achieve its aims by creating a climate of fear. Every year it kidnaps hundreds of people, especially employees of foreign corporations, and it frequently attacks the country's oil pipelines. In 1999, the ELN forced the Colombian government to negotiate with it by conducting a campaign of mass kidnappings, including several US citizens.

weblinks

For a short history of terrorism since the twelfth century go to
www.waylinks.co.uk/
21debatesterrorism

VIEWPOINT

'If the spring of popular government in time of peace is virtue, the springs of popular government in revolution are at once virtue and terror: virtue, without which terror is fatal; terror, without which virtue is powerless. Terror is nothing other than justice, prompt, severe, inflexible...'
From a speech by Maximilien Robespierre, 1794

The origins of terrorism

Terrorism has occurred throughout history and in all parts of the world. It has been practised by small or weak groups as a means of attacking governments, and by governments themselves as a means of suppressing opposition. In the first century AD, Roman emperors such as Tiberius and Caligula used banishment, confiscation of property and execution to discourage opposition to their rule. The word 'assassin' originated from an eleventh-century secret society in Persia (present-day Iran), known as the Order of Assassins, who carried out murders of high-ranking politicians and military leaders.

However, terrorism was not used methodically, as an instrument of state policy, until the French Revolution at the end of the eighteenth century. During the Reign of Terror (1793-4), hundreds of suspected counter-revolutionaries were sent to the guillotine, creating a climate of fear among the general population. This policy was openly adopted by the revolutionary leader Maximilien Robespierre as a means of suppressing all opposition. The word 'terrorism' made its first appearance in 1795.

Terror tactics were used in the latter half of the nineteenth century by anarchist groups in Europe, Russia and America, who believed they could bring about political change by assassinating people in positions of power. However, during this period and until well into the twentieth century, most of the terrorism in the world was inflicted by governments.

Terrorism in the twentieth century

In the twentieth century, terrorism became the tool of totalitarian regimes. For example, after the Bolsheviks won control of Russia in the 1917 revolution, their leader, Vladimir Lenin, founded a secret police force called the Cheka that used terror to enforce his party's grip on power. The role of the secret police was expanded under Lenin's successor, Joseph Stalin. The Gestapo was used in similar ways in Nazi Germany (1933-1945); during the Second World War, French, Czech and Polish resistance movements who carried out ambushes, sabotage, and assassinations, were seen as terrorists by the Nazi occupiers of Europe.

Nationalist movements rose up after the war with the aim of ousting colonial powers from their homelands. For example, the Viet Minh of Vietnam carried out random shootings and bomb attacks in order to demoralize the French occupiers. In Palestine, Jewish militant groups, like Irgun and Stern, aimed to force the British out of Palestine by blowing up hotels and ambushing British army patrols.

The Irgun's ammunition ship Altalena on fire off the Tel Aviv beach, following a fight between commandos of the Irgun terrorist organization and the Israeli Army. The incident began when the Jewish militants refused to surrender the ship to the Israeli Government.

Modern terrorism

The success of groups like the Viet Minh, Irgun, and the FLN, were the inspiration for modern terrorism. This began in 1968 when violent terrorist groups arose in places like West Germany, Italy and Japan, attacking what they saw as the 'fascist capitalism' – exploitation of the working classes by rich businesses – of their homelands. In America an extreme anti-war group called the Weathermen, opposing their country's involvement in Vietnam, planted bombs in government buildings.

At the 1972 Olympic Games in Munich, a Palestinian terrorist group, known as Black September, killed two Israeli athletes and seized eleven more. Here one of the Arab gunmen appears on a balcony at the Israeli team's quarters. Later, in a botched rescue attempt, nine more Israeli athletes and five terrorists were killed.

The most significant and lasting terrorist group formed in the 1960s was the Palestine Liberation Organization (PLO), a movement representing the Palestinian people, dedicated to the destruction of Israel, because they saw Israelis as occupiers of their homeland. In 1967, the PLO decided to adopt terrorist tactics. A year later the Irish Republican Army (IRA), a long-established paramilitary group of Irish nationalists opposing British rule

in Northern Ireland, also recommenced their
terrorist campaign.

In other parts of the world, such as Malaysia,
Indonesia, the Philippines, Argentina and El
Salvador, revolutionary groups entered into violent
conflict with established governments. Many were
inspired by the teachings of communist thinkers
such as Marx, Lenin and Mao, and they wished
to bring about communist revolutions in their
own countries.

During the Cold War (1945-1990), when the
communist Soviet Union (present-day Russia) and
its allies confronted the USA and the capitalist
West, several of these groups were given financial
and military aid by the Soviet Union. Similarly,
radical left-wing groups in Europe were given
weapons, false passports and shelter by communist
East Germany.

A number of these groups held extreme views far
outside the political mainstream. With the ending
of the Cold War, and the consequent loss of
support, many of these post-1968 terrorist groups
faded out of existence. The ones that have
survived, such as the PLO and the IRA, have done
so because their movements sprang from more
deep-rooted, popular grievances – the perceived
loss or occupation of their homeland.

Since the 1980s, one of the most dominant forces
behind international terrorism has been Islamic
fundamentalism. The Islamic revolution in Iran in
1979 (see page 18), together with the on-going
grievances of the Palestinians and other Muslim
peoples, has led to a huge growth in Islamic
terrorist organizations, funded by countries like
Iran, Saudi Arabia, Libya and Iraq, and full of
hatred towards Israel and its supporters in the
West.

DEBATE

Are terrorist acts ever
justifiable? Should
people who engage in
political violence be
judged by their aims or
by their methods?

THE ROOTS OF TERRORISM

What drives people to kill for a cause?

People turn to terrorism for many different reasons. They may wish to free their country from foreign rule or a repressive regime, or they may see terrorism as a means of bringing about a religious or political revolution. Most terrorist groups have a grievance of some kind. They are usually a subgroup of a larger population, for example an ethnic minority who feel that they have been treated unjustly.

People who, because of their economic situation, race, religion, or political views, are denied a voice in the politics of their country, can become angry and frustrated. A number of factors may then

Palestinian youths fire slingshots at Israeli soldiers during clashes over disputed territory. Some Palestinians feel drawn to violent resistance because of anger at the loss of their homeland.

trigger the move towards violence, such as impatience with the slowness of the political process in bringing about a desired change. (This was the case with many of the terrorist groups in Europe and Japan in the late 1960s and early 1970s.) Another reason might be a sense that a particular moment in history presents a unique opportunity, as in the IRA's campaign against a weakened Britain after the First World War, and Irgun's attacks on the British in Palestine after the Second World War. Groups can also be encouraged by the success of other similar organizations – as the post-1968 terrorists were undoubtedly inspired by the FLN in Algeria.

Rebels with a cause

What sort of people become terrorists? There is no single terrorist personality type. Terrorists come from a wide range of social and educational backgrounds, although nowadays most terrorist leaders tend to be well-educated and either middle-class or upper-class. In 1978, a West German psychiatrist who examined four members of the Red Army Faction terrorist gang (a small, West-German, pro-communist terrorist group which emerged out of the 1960s protest movement) concluded that they were intelligent, even humorous, and showed no signs of psychosis.

What unites all members of such terrorist groups is their fanaticism, a trait that is intensified by the isolated and dangerous lives they lead. Their powerful commitment to a cause tends to override other human qualities such as pity or fear. The mutual reassurance, strength and comradeship found in these groups tends to reinforce terrorists in their extreme views.

Andreas Baader who, with Ulrike Meinhof, formed a violent left-wing terrorist gang in Germany in 1970.

VIEWPOINT

'Terrorists seldom demand the full realization of their cause, possibly because they don't expect it, but equally probably ... because achieving their goals would force them to relinquish their accumulated power.... Frequently, therefore, when a cause is realized ... terrorists continue to operate but change their causes. German student terrorists, for example, began as an anti-Vietnam War movement. After the war, they took up other causes.'
L. John Martin, Professor Emeritus, College of Journalism, University of Maryland, USA

A mural in West Belfast supporting the IRA, a militant nationalist group. Until their ceasefire in 1997, the IRA used violence in an attempt to end British rule in Northern Ireland.

Nationalism

A major cause of terrorism over the past hundred years has been nationalism: the belief of a people with a common cultural or ethnic background in their right to form their own nation. Nationalism has been a powerful rallying cry for people whose countries have been conquered or colonized by foreign powers, or who have been forced to leave their homeland. As part of their fight for national liberation, many groups have turned to terrorism as a means of focusing the world's attention on their plight.

Early nationalist terrorist groups included the Irish IRA, the Jewish Irgun and the Algerian FLN, who sought to expel colonial rulers from their land. Others followed, including the PLO, and Basque Fatherland and Liberty (ETA), a movement founded with the aim of establishing a separate state in northern Spain.

Nationalist terrorists have been more successful than other types of terrorist group in achieving at least some of their aims. This may be because the great powers in the world are also nation-states, and can sympathize with a people's desire for self-determination. The FLN and Irgun won their respective struggles against colonial rule; and the IRA has won concessions from the British government and has now started to enter the mainstream through its political wing, Sinn Fein.

Ideology

Ideology, a system of political beliefs, has been a strong motivation for terrorism since the nineteenth century. There are three major strands of ideological terrorism: anarchist, right-wing, and left-wing. Anarchists reject the idea that society requires a system of government and believe that government should be abolished. Anarchist terrorism was at its height from the 1870s until about 1920. During this time anarchist revolutionaries were responsible for a wave of bombings and assassinations. One victim was the US president William McKinley, killed in 1901 by a young Hungarian refugee with anarchist sympathies. Some see the recent rise of violent protests against capitalism and globalization, for example at the Seattle World Trade Organization Ministerial Conference in November and December 1999, as a revival of anarchist terrorism.

FACT

The PKK (Kurdistan Workers Party) is a nationalist terrorist group dedicated to the establishment of an independent Kurdistan. Its chief target is Turkey, where nearly half the world's Kurdish population lives; many Kurdish civilians have suffered forcible displacement and sometimes torture at the hands of the Turkish government. The PKK have caused an estimated 10,000 deaths since 1990.

Two Kurdish PKK members, captured by Turkish soldiers. Apart from their conflict with the Turks, the Kurds have also suffered at the hands of Iraqi leader Saddam Hussein who has used the Kurdish people to test the effects of his biological and chemical weapons.

A Ku Klux Klan rally in Pittsburgh, USA, in 1998. The KKK are a white-supremacist group who gained their greatest following in the southern USA during the 1920s.

Right-wing terrorism is practised by extremist groups who are motivated by a fear of social change and multiculturalism. They are usually highly patriotic, racist, and opposed to socialist or liberal democratic forms of government. These views are most often associated with fascism, which achieved its greatest popularity between the 1920s and 1940s, when fascist terror was practised both by governments in Germany and Italy, and by right-wing groups in other parts of Europe. Right-wing terrorism declined after 1945, although fascist neo-Nazi and white-supremacist groups have continued to carry out occasional attacks on immigrants and refugees in Western Europe and the USA.

Left-wing terrorists seek to destroy the capitalist economic system, which they believe is responsible for all the poverty and inequality in the world, and replace it with a socialist or communist form of government. Left-wing terrorists first emerged in 1968 after a wave of student riots around the world, and they were most active during the 1970s and 1980s. Such groups included the Baader-Meinhof Group from Germany, the Japanese Red Army, the Weathermen in the USA, and the Red Brigades of Italy.

weblinks

For more information about the Baader-Meinhof Group, the Japanese Red Army and the Italian Red Brigades go to www.waylinks.co.uk/ 21debatesterrorism

Religion

In recent years there has been a growth of extremist groups on the fringes of certain religions. These religious terrorists justify their use of violence by viewing it as the will of God. They see themselves as instruments of divine justice, righting the wrongs of the world and destroying the enemies of their faith.

Towards the end of the twentieth century, militant Christian sects warned of a final showdown between the forces of good and evil, causing fears of terrorist attacks at the turn of the millennium. Fortunately, such attacks did not occur. Radical Jewish groups include the followers of the late Rabbi Meir Kahane, who advocated the expulsion of all Arabs from Israel. The Aum Shinrikyo cult in Japan could also be classified as a religious terrorist group. Its members believed they could save the world from imminent destruction by transferring evil energy into positive energy through meditation and by remaining isolated from the world. Aum Shinrikyo were responsible for launching a deadly gas attack in the Tokyo subway in 1995, killing twelve people and injuring 5,000.

VIEWPOINTS

'... the so-called peaceful solutions, and the international conferences to solve the Palestinian problem, are all contrary to the beliefs of the Islamic Resistance Movement. For renouncing any part of Palestine means renouncing part of the religion ... There is no solution to the Palestinian problem except by *Jihad* [holy war]...'
Excerpt from the charter of terrorist group, HAMAS

'Confronting and ending terrorism are indispensable steps on the road to peace. In my meetings with Chairman Arafat I made it clear that he and the Palestinian Authority could no longer equivocate. They must decide as the rest of the world has decided that terrorism must end.'
US Secretary of State Colin Powell, April 2002

Passengers await medical treatment after being evacuated from the Tokyo Subway following the Aum Shinrikyo gas attack in March 1995.

weblinks►

For an in-depth article about Islamic fundamentalism and Islamic terrorism go to www.waylinks.co.uk/ 21debatesterrorism

Far more numerous are the radical Islamic groups. According to *The Economist* magazine, Muslims were responsible for eleven or possibly twelve out of sixteen major acts of terrorism between 1983 and 2000. Muslim groups have been involved in terrorist attacks in Asia, the Far East, the Middle East, North Africa and Europe. They include the al Qaida network, which finances and trains Islamic militants worldwide, and HAMAS, a Palestinian Sunni Muslim organization that has carried out many attacks on Israel. The strength of these groups and the wealth of their supporters have enabled them to extend their attacks well beyond national boundaries.

Many of these attacks have been against Western targets. Yet, only a hundred years ago, Islam and the West co-existed peacefully. In the Muslim Ottoman Empire, Jews and Christians were given full religious freedom, and in Muslim Jerusalem – now a bitterly contested city – Jews, Christians and Muslims lived together in reasonable harmony. In most parts of the world, this remains the case. The vast majority of Muslims, like people of all faiths, wish to live in peace with their fellow human beings. However, for a vocal minority, the West came to be seen as the enemy.

The foundation of Israel in 1948 caused much hostility, which was heightened by continued Western – particularly American – support for the Jewish state. However, Islamic terrorism really began after the 1979 Iranian revolution that brought to power a fundamentalist Islamic government. This led to a revival of Islamic fundamentalism, preaching strict observance of the laws of Islam's holy book, the *Qu'ran*, and hostile to the values and culture of the West which were seen as sinful and decadent. Some radical Muslim groups began to call for a *jihad* or 'holy war' against

Anti-US demonstrators burn the American flag in Lahore, Pakistan, shortly after the 11 September attacks. Americans suffered terrorist attacks long before 2001. In March 1995, two US Embassy officials were murdered in Pakistan.

the West, and the terrorists saw themselves leading the attack.

A powerful element driving Islamic terrorism today is anti-Americanism. The USA has had friendly relations with Islam in the past, supporting Arab Islamic groups in the 1950s and 1960s in their struggle against the Egyptian government. The USA also helped Muslim minorities in Bosnia and Kosovo when they were threatened by Serbia during the 1990s. However, America's ongoing support for Israel, its stationing of a large military force in Muslim Saudi Arabia during the Gulf War of 1990-1, and its bombing campaign in Iraq during the last decade, has enraged Muslim radicals, and led many to join terrorist organizations.

VIEWPOINTS

'It is evil that causes terrorism but the evil needs to spread its ideology as a mass base and the best breeding ground is poverty.'
President Gloria Arroyo of the Philippines, 2001

'If the liberal worldview was correct [that poverty causes terrorism], Saudis should be the most peaceable people on earth. They are well-educated and well-fed by the state, which can afford such generosity thanks to the fortuitous location of large deposits of oil. And to be sure, most Saudis are peaceable. But their system also has created a breeding ground for terrorists like Osama bin Laden, who was born into wealth and privilege in Saudi Arabia. He is proof that it is not poverty that causes terrorism.'
Bruce Bartlett, National Center for Policy Analysis, USA, 2001

Poverty and deprivation

It has been argued by many that a root cause of terrorism is the growing inequality between rich and poor, and that young people from developing countries, frustrated by their lot and resentful of the rich West, are increasingly attracted to radical and violent causes. According to the US State Department's annual human rights report of March 2002, terrorist groups have been gaining followers among citizens of countries who 'lack economic opportunity'. However, there is little evidence to point to a strong link between poverty and terrorism.

Between 1996 and 1999, Nasra Hassan, a United Nations relief worker, interviewed nearly 250 people involved in suicide attacks, including failed bombers and families of dead bombers. She found that 'none of them were uneducated, desperately poor, simple-minded or depressed.' The nineteen terrorists who carried out the attacks against targets in the USA on 11 September 2001 were all college-educated and from middle-class families.

A high illiteracy rate is one sign of a country's poverty, yet the countries regarded as sponsors of terrorism have an average illiteracy rate of 17 per cent, the same as the worldwide rate. Many countries which suffer from terrorism, such as Ireland or Spain, are not poor. The evidence suggests that poorer countries with strong ethnic or religious divisions are more likely to suffer from civil war than terrorism.

The media

One of the main goals of terrorism is to attract publicity for its cause. The media are essential to terrorism because they bring the identities, activities and demands of terrorists to the attention of the world. In this sense it can be argued that the

Police and emergency workers look on as a fire engulfs the Sari nightclub in the popular tourist resort of Kuta Beach, Bali, following the terrorist bomb attack on 12 October 2002. The attack was blamed on local Islamic terrorists, with possible links to al Qaida.

media are one cause of terrorism; if terrorist activities stopped being reported, terrorism as we know it would quickly cease to exist. It cannot be denied that the media – both television and newspapers – have a powerful interest in reporting terrorism. It provides them with the drama, conflict, suspense and powerful visual images that make a good news story.

From the terrorists' point of view, the media's coverage of an incident such as a hijacking, a kidnapping, or a hostage-taking, makes the whole action worthwhile. The fact that they rarely achieve their demands, such as the release of prisoners, is less important to them than the fact that their cause has been publicized.

DEBATE

Should journalists continue to inform the public about terrorist attacks, or is this simply playing into the hands of the terrorists?

VIEWPOINTS

'Let me put forward the proposition that the media, particularly television, and terrorists need one another.... Without television, terrorism becomes rather like the philosopher's hypothetical tree falling in the forest: no one hears it fall and therefore it has no reason for being. And television without terrorism, while not deprived of all interesting things in the world, is nonetheless deprived of one of the most interesting.'
Ted Koppel, ABC anchor

'We present facts from which people draw their own conclusions ... whether it's politics or terrorists or anything else.... If we start playing God and say that fact or this viewpoint ... might give people ideas, we would have to stop covering politics.'
Richard Salant, president of CBS News

One reason why Western Europe has been a favourite target of terrorist attacks is because terrorists know they will receive more media coverage than they would for similar attacks in other parts of the world. Some terrorist groups, like the Red Brigades in Italy, even timed their activities for Wednesdays and Saturdays so as to get themselves into the bigger Thursday and Sunday newspapers.

State-sponsored terrorism

During the second half of the twentieth century, certain countries found it was in their interests to forge secret connections with terrorist organizations. They provided these organizations

Soviet and East German troops crush an uprising in East Berlin in 1953. The same East German government was happy to support anti-American terrorist groups abroad, such as the Red Army Faction in West Germany.

with financial and political support, weaponry, training and sometimes shelter. State sponsorship and funding have allowed organizations to carry out more ambitious attacks, such as hijackings and aeroplane bombings. In return, the terrorist organization provided the sponsoring states with a means of indirectly launching attacks on their enemies and spreading their ideological or religious beliefs without any outward sign of their involvement.

For example, during the Cold War, the Soviet Union and its East European allies sponsored left-wing terrorist groups in many parts of the world. Sponsored groups included the Red Brigades, the Red Army Faction and ETA in Europe, the PLO in the Middle East, the Japanese Red Army, and the National Liberation Army (ELN) in Bolivia. Similarly, the American Central Intelligence Agency (CIA) provided support and training for counter-revolutionary groups in places like South Vietnam, Cuba, Guatemala, Nicaragua, Argentina and Chile. In this way, the superpowers were able to wage a proxy war without having to risk outright confrontation.

Since the end of the Cold War, state sponsorship of terrorism has declined. However, according to the US State Department, there are seven countries which continue to be major sponsors of terrorism today. These are Iran, Iraq, Syria, Libya, Cuba, North Korea, and Sudan. The Americans claim that Iran is the most active state sponsor of terrorism, providing support to many groups, including the Lebanese Hizbollah, and the Palestinian groups HAMAS and the Palestine Islamic Jihad (PIJ). The same source claims that Cuba has links with two Colombian terrorist organizations, and has sheltered several terrorists, including members of ETA.

FACT

Terrorists who lack a state sponsor find their own ways of raising funds. These can include ransoms from kidnappings, or the proceeds of bank robberies, drug dealing and various forms of organized crime. Many Islamic terrorist groups rely on donations from wealthy religious Muslims, as well as from collections in mosques. These come to them via some Muslim charities. For example, the 1993 World Trade Center bombing was partly financed by money that came from the Alkifah Refugee Center in Brooklyn, New York

weblinks

For more information about state-sponsored terrorism go to www.waylinks.co.uk/ 21debatesterrorism

TERRORIST GROUPS

Who are the major terrorist groups at work in the world today and how did they develop? This chapter looks at the aims of these organizations, and the methods they use to fulfil those aims.

Palestine Liberation Organization (PLO)

The Palestinians have been a stateless people since 1948, when the state of Israel was founded in the territory that had been their homeland. The PLO was founded in 1964 as a nationalist movement representing the large numbers of Palestinians living in refugee camps in Lebanon. Soon afterwards the group split into different factions, each with their own views on how to achieve the ultimate goal of re-establishing a Palestinian state. The factions included the Popular Front for the Liberation of Palestine, the Popular Democratic Front for the Liberation of Palestine, and al-Fatah. However, each of these groups remained part of the PLO organization.

Following the disastrous defeat of the Arab forces by Israel in the Six Day War of 1967, Israel occupied new territories in the West Bank and Gaza Strip. Nearly 400,000 Palestinians were forced back into Jordan. Here the PLO regrouped and decided to adopt terrorist tactics to attain their new goal: the destruction of the state of Israel. And they chose a new leader: Yasser Arafat. The following year they began a campaign of air piracy by hijacking an Israeli passenger plane and forcing it to land in Algeria. From Jordan they carried out border raids into Israel. In 1970 the Palestinians and the PLO were expelled from Jordan. They then

moved to southern Lebanon, where they continued to raid and shell northern Israel.

In 1974, the PLO decided to alter its strategy from one of pure terrorism, and look at political ways of advancing its cause. At the Arab League conference at Rabat in Morocco that year, the PLO was given official recognition by the United Nations and by the Arab peoples as the representative organization of the Palestinians. By this means, Arafat managed to change the image of the PLO from a group of ruthless terrorists to a movement with legitimate claims.

A hijacked plane is blown up in Jordan, 1970, by the Popular Front for the Liberation of Palestine – an offshoot of the PLO. This action led to the expulsion of the PLO from Jordan.

weblinks

For a brief history of the
Arab-Israeli conflict go to
www.waylinks.co.uk/
21debatesterrorism

In 1982, Israeli forces moved into southern Lebanon, forcing the PLO to retreat from their bases there. Arafat caused major splits in the PLO when he decided soon afterwards to engage in peace talks with the Israelis. These talks failed, but by 1988 Arafat had gone further and publicly admitted that Israel had the right to exist. He also announced the end of the PLO's terrorist campaign.

These moves led to the first serious peace negotiations between the two sides, resulting in the Oslo Accord and the 1993 Declaration of Principles signed in Washington DC. The Palestinians were granted partial self-government of territories in the West Bank and the Gaza Strip as a step towards a fully independent Palestine. Two groups within the PLO left the parent organization in protest at this treaty and continued their terrorist campaign, while many young Palestinians became impatient with the slowness of progress, and joined more radical organizations.

In 2000 Israel provoked an *intifada* (uprising) by the Palestinians when it occupied Palestinian settlements in the West Bank and Gaza. In 2002 the peace process came under severe threat as the PLO failed to control the violence of these radical groups and Israel adopted an even more aggressive policy by bombing Palestinian territories. Whether the PLO would be able to continue along the path of peaceful negotiation, or would make a return to its terrorist roots, was unclear.

Liberation Tigers of Tamil Eelam (LTTE)
The Tamil Tigers are a separatist movement aiming at establishing an independent state for the Tamil community in the north-east of Sri Lanka. They are also supported by some Tamils living in India. The LTTE was formed in 1976 and began its armed

FACT

The LTTE is the only terrorist group to have assassinated two heads of state. Members of its elite unit, the Black Tigers, carried out successful suicide bomb attacks against India's Prime Minister Rajiv Gandhi in 1991, and Sri Lanka's President Ranasinghe Premadasa in 1993.

conflict with the Sri Lankan government in 1983. It has used terrorism and guerilla warfare (armed struggle by a revolutionary force against the armed forces of a government) as well as full-scale conventional warfare. The LTTE have been based in north-eastern Sri Lanka, and at the peak of their campaign they controlled most of the northern and eastern coastal areas.

The LTTE's terrorist activities have included assassinations of political and military leaders and bombings throughout the island of Sri Lanka. At its height, the organization was estimated to have between 8,000 and 10,000 armed members, with a core of trained soldiers, numbering between 3,000 and 6,000, known as the Black Tigers.

weblinks

For more information about the LTTE go to www.waylinks.co.uk/ 21debatesterrorism

A member of the Tamil Tigers aims his machine gun during exercises in eastern Sri Lanka in 1995. At this time the LTTE was recruiting children as young as fourteen.

Peace talks between the LTTE and the Sri Lankan government began in 1985, with India acting as mediator. An accord was signed in 1987, and the LTTE handed over a large portion of its weaponry. However, the accord collapsed later that year and the conflict resumed. A ceasefire was agreed in 1989, but subsequent peace talks failed and the government declared war on the LTTE in 1990. Another round of negotiations failed in 1994-5, and the LTTE continued with their guerilla campaign as well as terrrorist bomb attacks against government buildings, banks, ships, trains, buses and power stations.

In early 2002, the Sri Lankan government and the Tamil Tigers agreed to another ceasefire as part of a new peace initiative negotiated with the help of the Norwegian government. The war-weary people on both sides were hoping that almost two decades of war, in which over 64,000 people have died, might finally end.

Provisional Irish Republican Army (IRA)

The IRA was formed by radical Irish Catholics after the First World War, with the aim of removing the British from Ireland. Their assassination campaign led to British reprisals and a bloody war between 1919 and 1921. After the war, Ireland was split into two parts – Protestant Ulster, in the north, and the Catholic south (which became the Republic of Ireland in 1949). This division was bitterly opposed by the IRA, who continued to mount occasional attacks in Northern Ireland and the British mainland for the next forty years.

The conflict escalated in 1968-9 when a civil rights movement protesting at the treatment of Catholics in Northern Ireland clashed with

VIEWPOINT

'I believe it is a just and Christian thing to try and overthrow tyranny ... and the British government have tyrannized Ireland. While it exists it is the duty of every Irishman to try and overthrow this tyranny, and I believe I have done my duty to my country.'
IRA member, Gerard Lyons, in 1939, on being sentenced to twenty years in prison for bomb attacks in London

Flames from a petrol bomb blaze in a street in Londonderry, Northern Ireland, at the start of 'the Troubles' in 1969.

Protestant street gangs. A split in the IRA led to the formation of a radical splinter group, the Provisional IRA, committed to a strategy of violence and terrorism against the British 'occupiers'. The Provos were the armed wing of the political party, Sinn Fein, which used the available political institutions to further the cause of Irish independence.

Between 1969 and 1994, the Provisional IRA waged a campaign of bombings, assassinations and kidnappings. Their targets included pubs, stations and shopping centres in mainland Britain, and British military and Ulster police targets in Northern Ireland.

weblinks

For more information about the IRA go to www.waylinks.co.uk/ 21debatesterrorism

In 2001, British Prime Minister Tony Blair meets his Irish counterpart Bertie Ahern to finalize a deal to rescue the Good Friday Agreement.

The IRA membership numbers in the hundreds; they are organized into small, tightly-knit cells under the leadership of an Army Council. They have received funding and aid from sympathetic groups in the USA, and have received weapons and training in Libya and from the PLO.

Peace talks between the IRA and the British government began in secret in the early 1990s, leading to an IRA ceasefire in 1994. Impatience at the lack of progress led to a brief renewal of the bombing campaign in 1996-7. Then, in 1998, the so-called Good Friday Agreement was signed. Sinn Fein were invited to join a new Northern Ireland executive committee, political prisoners were to be released, and the IRA were required to 'place their weapons beyond use'.

This agreement was widely supported in Ireland, but sparked opposition from radical groups on both sides. It led to the formation of the Real IRA, which continued the terrorist campaign. The Provisional IRA began decommissioning small parts of its arsenal in 2001.

Basque Homeland and Freedom (ETA)

The Basque are a stateless people living in the western Pyrenees, in north-eastern Spain and south-western France. Euskadi Ta Askatasuna (ETA) was founded in 1959 by young Basque activists disillusioned with the moderate stance of the traditional Basque nationalist party, the Partido Nacionalista Vasco. ETA's aim was and remains the creation of an independent Basque nation in north-eastern Spain.

It launched its campaign in 1959 with bomb attacks on the Spanish cities of Bilbao, Vitoria and Santander. The repressive measures employed by the police, including torture, drove many Basque

weblinks

For more information about ETA go to
www.waylinks.co.uk/
21debatesterrorism

separatists abroad, but also led many more to join the struggle. From 1968, ETA was responsible for a string of assassinations, mostly of government officials, military leaders, judges and politicians. After 1976, the Basque region in Spain was granted its own parliament with tax-raising powers, and given control over its schools, where the Basque language and culture began to be taught.

However the hardline terrorists of ETA were not satisfied, and continued to demand full independence. They intensified their attacks against security forces and politicians, including fellow Basques who they believed had betrayed the cause. In 1980, ETA's bloodiest year, the group killed 118 people.

VIEWPOINTS

'The process that started last year is blocked and poisoned, and in that context, Euskadi Ta Askatasuna has made the decision to reactivate its armed struggle ... and we call on the Basque people to continue their work of nation-building, facing up [to] the enemy and reinforcing the basic pillars of our nation.'
From an ETA communiqué, 1999

'ETA is wrong again when it doesn't hear society's call for peace and for living together peacefully. ETA is wrong again if it thinks that with coercion, with blackmail and with terror, it will cause a breakdown in democracy and freedom.'
Spanish Prime Minister Jose Maria Aznar, responding to ETA's decision to end its ceasefire, 1999

Firemen inspect a damaged department store near where a car bomb exploded in central Madrid in July 2000. The attack, attributed to ETA, slightly injured six people.

Peace talks were held in 1992 between the Spanish government and ETA, but these came to nothing. Influenced by the IRA, ETA announced a ceasefire in 1998, although small-scale attacks continued in the Basque region. In December 1999, ETA resumed its terrorist campaign, blaming repressive measures taken by the Spanish authorities and the failure of other Basque nationalists to work with it. So far, in more than forty years of violence, the organization has killed more than 800 people.

ETA is believed to have no more than twenty activists and a few hundred supporters. Its headquarters are in the Basque regions of Spain and France, with overseas support in Europe, Latin America and Africa. ETA members have received training in the past in Libya, South Yemen, Lebanon and Nicaragua. It is funded by Basque supporters, drug smuggling, kidnap ransoms and robbery. Like the IRA, the organization is structured in small, semi-independent cells, with only loose links to the leadership, making it difficult for Spanish government forces to penetrate.

Sendero Luminoso (Shining Path)

Shining Path is a left-wing terrorist organization based in Peru and formed in the late 1960s by the former university professor Abimael Guzman. It aims to destroy the existing economic and political institutions of Peru and replace them with a 'peasant revolutionary regime' like the one formed by the Chinese communist leader, Chairman Mao. It has attracted support in rural areas through its use of native Indian names and symbols.

Shining Path is regarded as one of the most brutal terrorist organizations in the world. Since it began its armed struggle in 1980, it has been responsible for the deaths of approximately 30,000 people.

Its activities include assassinations and planting bombs in crowded areas with little concern for the numbers of casualties. One of its aims is the removal of all foreign business interests from Peru, and since 1986, when it brought its campaign into Peruvian cities, it has attacked several foreign embassies and US businesses.

In 1991, the Peruvian government awarded itself emergency powers to deal more effectively with the threat from Shining Path, including the power to arrest, imprison, torture and execute suspected terrorists. The result has been the capture of over 2,500 Shining Path terrorists, including Guzman himself in 1992.

Abimael Guzman, leader of Shining Path, is guarded by special forces during his transfer to another prison in Lima, Peru, in 1993.

VIEWPOINTS

'From inside a cage where the government was attempting to humiliate him and the entire revolution before the press, [Guzman] disparaged his imprisonment as simply "a bend in the road". He defiantly called for the People's War to continue, declaring "Though the road is long, we shall travel it to the end. We will reach our goal and we will win."'
From the website of the Committee to Support the Revolution in Peru, 2001

'In 1992, when I was in Chile, I heard the terrible news of Maria Elena Moyano's murder. I still can't recover from the shock, sorrow, and fury. She was a wonderful woman and I loved her. The fact that they blasted her body after killing her shows there was far more than a "political judgement" against her. ...definitely something of a darker psychological nature was at stake there.'
Yolanda Sala, a Peruvian journalist, on the death of the human rights activist, Maria Elena Moyano, at the hands of the Shining Path

weblinks

For more information about Shining Path go to www.waylinks.co.uk/21debatesterrorism

The Peruvian president Alberto Fujimori granted an amnesty in 1995 to terrorists who surrendered, encouraging many to desert the cause. A weakened Shining Path, under the leadership of Oscar Ramirez Durand, continues to clash with the Peruvian military in the countryside, and sometimes carries out raids on villages.

At its height Shining Path had between 1,500 and 2,500 armed activists, and a larger number of supporters mainly in rural areas. However, its strength has been greatly reduced by arrests and desertions. In 2002 its armed membership numbered between 100 and 200. It is funded by robbery, drug trafficking, and an unofficial 'war tax' that it demands from rural businesses and individuals.

Al Qaida (The Base)

Al Qaida is an Islamic fundamentalist organization which finances, trains, equips and coordinates the activities of Islamic terrorists around the world. It was founded in Afghanistan in 1988, during the 1979-1989 war against the Soviet Union, and its

weblinks

For more information about al Qaida's origins go to www.waylinks.co.uk/21debatesterrorism

Osama bin Laden at a news conference in April 1998 in which he called for a holy war against the USA.

core members are veterans of that war. It is led by Osama bin Laden, a wealthy, charismatic Muslim from Saudi Arabia. A sophisticated communications network connects bin Laden to his followers all over the Arab world, as well as in Europe, Asia and North America.

Bin Laden moved to Afghanistan in 1979, the year of the Soviet invasion, and set up a recruiting and training office, Maktab al-Khidamat (MAK), which advertised all over the Islamic world for conscripts to come and help repel the invaders. He also brought in experts on guerilla warfare and covert operations. Nearly 10,000 volunteers were trained in MAK camps, arriving from Saudi Arabia, Algeria, Egypt, Yemen, Pakistan and Sudan.

MAK was one of seven main groups forming the Mujahedin, the guerilla force that fought the *jihad*, or holy war, against the Soviet Union. Several of these factions, including bin Laden's, were given weapons and training by the USA to help them in their fight against the USA's Cold War enemy. Towards the end of the war, bin Laden set up al Qaida to further the Islamic cause in other parts of the world.

Afghan soldiers during the war against the Soviet Union. During the 1980s thousands of volunteers came from the Middle East to Afghanistan to help their fellow Muslims. These Afghan-Arab Mujahedin were crucial in the victory over Soviet forces.

FACT

It has been estimated that at least 70,000 Islamic extremists have received terrorist training at al Qaida camps.

TERRORISM

What characteristics do the world's major terrrorist organzations have in common?

The experience of the Afghan war, which bin Laden saw as a war between believers and heretics, greatly influenced the outlook of those who formed the core of al Qaida. They adopted a new, very strict and warlike version of Islam, emphasizing the virtues of *jihad* and martyrdom and downgrading the role of women.

A body is carried from the wreckage following a bomb attack near the US embassy in Nairobi, Kenya, in August 1998. The bomb, planted by members of al Qaida, killed 158 people and left 4,824 injured.

Despite the help they received from the USA during that conflict, they came to see the West, and Western culture, as profoundly opposed to their way of life. The USA, because of its power and influence, was viewed as the prime enemy of Islam, and during the 1990s bin Laden issued three *fatwahs* (religious rulings) calling upon Muslims to take up arms against America. Al Qaida see the current governments of all Islamic states as corrupt, heretical and Western-influenced. The group's primary goals are to spread their version of Islam, to destroy American interests in the Middle East, to overthrow the existing governments of the Muslim states, and to replace them with leaders who rule according to fundamentalist Islamic law.

Al Qaida has semi-independent terrorist cells or groups in more than fifty countries around the world, coordinated by its base. Until 2001, the al Qaida base was in Afghanistan, where it helped establish and support an Islamic fundamentalist regime, the Taliban. Because of its shadowy and dispersed nature it is not always easy to link al Qaida to specific terrorist attacks. However, its involvement is strongly suspected in a number of attacks within Arab countries, including bombings of hotels and government buildings in Yemen (1992), Saudi Arabia (1995 and 1996), and Pakistan (1995).

It was also almost certainly behind a number of attacks on American targets, including the bombing of the World Trade Center and an attack on American forces in Somalia (both in 1993). In addition, it was proved to be responsible for the bombing of American embassies in Kenya and Tanzania (1998). Most infamously, al Qaida was responsible for the attacks on targets within the USA on 11 September 2001 (see pages 46-51).

VIEWPOINTS

'Nothing is more sacred than belief except repulsing an enemy who is attacking religion and life. On that basis, and in compliance with God's order, we issue the following *fatwah* [ruling] to all Muslims. The ruling to kill the Americans and their allies – civilians and military – is an individual duty for every Muslim who can do it in any country in which it is possible to do it...'
Osama bin Laden, published in **Al-Quds al-'Arabi**, *1998*

'We condemn in the strongest terms possible what are apparently vicious and cowardly acts of terrorism against innocent civilians. We join with all Americans in calling for the swift apprehension and punishment of the perpetrators. No cause could ever be assisted by such immoral acts.'
Statement from Council on American-Islamic Relations (an Islamic organization), following attacks on 11 September 2001

RESPONSES TO TERRORISM

Military action or negotiation?

Difficult questions face countries targeted for terrorist attack. Should they respond with equal ferocity, using their armed forces and police to try to wipe out the terrorist threat? Or should they try to end the bloodshed by opening a dialogue with the terrorists, in the hope of finding a political solution to the conflict? Government responses differ, depending on the political character of the regime, the type of terrorism being practised, and the nature and popularity of the terrorist cause.

Taliban soldiers stand beside destroyed houses in an alleged terrorist camp which was hit by US missiles in Khost, eastern Afghanistan, September 1998. The missiles were launched in retaliation for bombings at US embassies in Kenya and Tanzania which killed 257 people.

Military action

Historically, governments have often chosen to take direct military action against the terrorists and those who support them. The main advantage of this strategy is that it sends a clear message to the target country's people, the victims of the assault and their families, the international community, and finally the terrorists themselves and their supporters, that the government is determined to defend itself against external or internal attack.

Sometimes this kind of action can be effective. For example, in 1986 the investigation into an attack on a West Berlin disco, in which two US soldiers died, revealed that the perpetrators had been trained in Libya. Then US President Ronald Reagan ordered an air strike on a number of targets in Libya, including terrorist training facilities. In the years following this attack Libya noticeably decreased its involvement in support of international terrorism.

Another obvious advantage of the use of force is that it can, if effective, damage or destroy the terrorists' organization. However it is unusual for terrorist groups to suffer outright defeat through government aggression. The organization of most terrorist groups into self-sufficient cells makes it very hard for governments to fight them with conventional arms. The removal of one cell does not necessarily impair the functioning of the rest of the group.

Despite its superficial appeal, there are many dangers in using force against terrorism. Firstly, it can play directly into the terrorists' hands. One of the main short-term aims of terrorist action is to provoke governments into a level of violent action that will lose them popular support and provoke sympathy for the terrorist cause.

Terrorists often place themselves within communities where they have strong support. In such a situation, it is difficult for armed forces to kill the terrorists without risking the deaths of innocent people, including women and children. Direct military action can therefore expose governments to accusations of brutality, and bring worldwide condemnation.

Military action against terrorists can create new martyrs for the cause. It can be argued that Israel's robust response to terrorist attacks over many years has led to the creation of new generations of even more militant young Palestinians, causing a seemingly endless cycle of violence.

Covert action

All governments of countries who suffer terrorist attacks engage in covert (or undercover) action to try to disrupt terrorist networks within their own borders. Intelligence services carry out surveillance on terrorist suspects. Action is taken to freeze their financial assets. Captured terrorists are put under pressure to inform on their colleagues.

Covert action has proved highly effective in non-democratic countries where less importance is placed on issues of civil liberties. For example, a major terrorist threat facing Iran in 1981 was eliminated in three months by a brutal secret service campaign, including the torture and killing of suspects.

However, democratic governments have to tread more carefully. The introduction of compulsory identity cards might make it harder for terrorists to live anonymously, but it also affects the lives of every innocent citizen. Likewise, civil liberties groups in Britain warn that introducing greater police powers to combat terrorism – such as

FACT

In September 2001 US President George W. Bush signed an order asking 5,000 US banks to halt all financial transactions involving twenty-seven known terrorist organizations.

telephone tapping, imprisoning suspects without trial, and placing limits on freedom of speech – might lead to a general expansion in the powers of the state in relation to the individual. They fear that future governments might use these powers to suppress political opposition, thus threatening democracy itself.

DEBATE

Does the threat of terrorism give governments the right to restrict people's liberty?

Negotiation

The idea of negotiating with terrorists is distasteful to many, especially those who have lost family or friends in terrorist attacks. However, negotiations do take place between governments and terrorist groups, although this is not always admitted in public. For example, there were secret talks between the British government and the IRA in the late 1980s and early 1990s, despite the government's stated policy of not negotiating with terrorists.

PLO Chairman Yasser Arafat and then Israeli Prime Minister Yitzhak Rabin with then US President Bill Clinton in Washington in September 1993. This handshake marked the signing of a peace accord between Israel and the PLO in September 1993.

FACT

FACT

France has been more prone to negotiate with terrorists than most Western countries. An example of this occurred in July 1997, when Chechen kidnappers seized a group of French and British citizens. By November, the French hostages had been released, while the two British hostages remained captive. It was rumoured that the French had given $3.5 million to the kidnappers.

The decision to engage in talks with terrorists partly depends on the political character of the government. Over the years, democratic governments, dependent on the support of an electorate who desire peace and freedom from terror, have proved more willing to negotiate than authoritarian regimes who lack such pressures.

There are also certain types of terrorist cause that are more susceptible to negotiated solutions. Nationalist terrorism, for example, is far more frequently responded to by negotiation, than ideological or religious terrorism. Nationalists have definable grievances (such as the loss of their homeland) that are often seen as justified by a significant proportion of the country's population, as well as the international community. Their goals also tend to be straightforward, and it is often possible for governments to go some way towards meeting them. For example, the British and Spanish governments have respectively granted Northern Ireland and the Basque region their own parliaments.

IRA sniper Michael Caraher walks from Northern Ireland's Maze Prison as part of the terms of the Good Friday Peace Agreement, 2000. He killed at least 12 members of the security forces, including British soldier Stephen Restorick, shot dead in South Armagh, in 1997.

New recruits to Hizbollah, a radical Islamic group based in Iran, listen to a speech by their leader during a ceremony in 2001. Such extremist religious groups are very unlikely to accept negotiated settlements with their enemies.

A policy of negotiation does have its drawbacks, however, as it can give the terrorists an added sense of their own power and significance. If they think that a government is willing to talk it might lead them to increase their demands. And, once a process of negotiation has been entered into, there is no knowing when or how it might end.

Sometimes a mixing of strategies is effective. For instance, the Italian authorities dealt successfully with the Red Brigades by a combination of negotiation and covert action. They agreed to some political reforms and promised to reduce the prison terms of captive terrorists, while also using covert means to penetrate Red Brigades ranks.

A terrorist group whose main motivation has been based on the idea that it is engaged in a battle against an evil regime, may find it hard to adapt to a situation where it finds itself involved in talks with that same regime. For example, the peace processes in Northern Ireland and in the Arab-Israeli conflict have led to splits in the ranks of the terrorists, and the formation of breakaway groups unable to stomach the idea of a negotiated settlement.

VIEWPOINT

'The insistence that a negotiated solution can end terrorism actually helps the terrorists... The enhanced respectability with which the terrorist is thereby invested gives him a foretaste of success and an encouragement to persevere.'
Conor Cruise O'Brien. 'Impediments and Prerequisites to Counter-Terrorism'. **The Atlantic Monthly**

International counter-terrorist measures

Since the 1990s, terrorism has become more globalized. Taking advantage of the latest communications technology, groups such as al Qaida are able to coordinate, plan and carry out attacks from remote locations. Terrorists also make use of the global banking system to hold, transfer, or launder their money. For this reason, countries are increasingly searching for international solutions in the struggle against terrorism.

British Foreign Secretary Jack Straw and US Secretary of State Colin Powell voting on a resolution during a UN Security Council meeting. In 2001 the UN established a counter-terrorism committee to monitor trends in terrorism and advise member states on how to avoid future terrorist attacks.

The United Nations (UN), an organization of states formed in 1945, at the end of the Second World War, to promote peace, security and international cooperation, has been the chief forum for international debates on terrorism since the 1960s. Over twenty major anti-terrorism resolutions and conventions have been passed by the UN in that time, committing signatories to specific measures against international terrorist activity. These include actions to prevent hijackings and hostage-taking, to protect heads of government or diplomats from assassination, and to guard against the financing of terrorism. The number of states that have signed these treaties varies greatly, from just twenty-five signatories for the agreement to protect diplomats, to 118 signatories for the treaty to suppress financing.

Resolution 1373, passed shortly after the terrorist attacks of 11 September 2001, called upon all states to work together to take action against terrorism, implementing bans on terrorist fundraising, recruitment to terrorist organizations, and the supply of weapons; the freezing of terrorist assets; the denial of a safe haven to those who finance, plan or commit terrorist acts; the use of border controls to restrict the movement of terrorists; and the provision of early warning of possible future terrorist acts to other countries.

Unfortunately, the political power of the UN is dwarfed by the power of its member states, who can ignore or sign up to the pledges as they please. These resolutions cannot be seen in themselves as a deterrent to terrorism. However, they do provide a legal framework for international cooperation, and they help to give legitimacy to actions taken by nations, individually or collectively, against terrorists.

weblinks

For details of UN action taken against terrorism go to www.waylinks.co.uk/21debatesterrorism

FACT

In February 2002, the European Union agreed to work towards adopting a common definition of terrorism ('Offenses intentionally committed by an individual or a group against one or more countries, their institutions or people, with the aim of intimidating them and seriously altering or destroying the political, economic, or social structures of a country'), common minimum penalties for those convicted of terrorism, greater intelligence sharing, and a Europe-wide arrest warrant to speed up extradition procedures for terrorist suspects.

THE TERRORIST ATTACK ON AMERICA

11 September 2001 and after

weblinks

For more information about the events of 11 September go to
www.waylinks.co.uk/terrorism

The events of Tuesday 11 September 2001 changed the world for ever. The most audacious terrorist attack ever planned was carried out against the world's most powerful nation.

At 8.45 a.m. a hijacked passenger airliner plunged into the north tower of the World Trade Center in New York City. Eighteen minutes later, a second hijacked plane crashed into the south tower, causing a massive explosion. At 9.43 a.m. American Airlines Flight 77 crashed into the Pentagon (the US Department of Defence) in Virginia. Soon afterwards, the two towers of the World Trade Center collapsed, sending a massive cloud of dust and debris through the streets of lower Manhattan. Finally, at 10.48 a.m. a fourth plane crashed in Pennsylvania, killing everyone on board. The hijackers of this last plane had been foiled in their attempt to crash it into another building – possibly the White House or Congress – when a group of passengers stormed the cockpit, and, it must be assumed, killed the terrorists.

The terrorists responsible were Islamic fundamentalists – almost certainly trained and coordinated by the al Qaida network. In the weeks that followed, as new information emerged, it became clear that 11 September had witnessed a

VIEWPOINT

'Of course it fell. It was the most awful, humbling, disgusting sight. All of a sudden, it was just a hundred-floor shaft of smoke. As it fell, as it was hitting the ground, the smoke and debris flew upward ... and the smoke arced away from the building in a series of neat, repulsively identical plumes. I looked at the center of the building and all I could see were a few scraggly black twisted girders pointing upward. Then they fell and it was all gone.'
Daniel Henninger, deputy editor at the **Wall Street Journal***, describing the fall of the north tower*

At 9.03 a.m. Flight 175 from Boston heads towards the south tower of the World Trade Center.

new level of terrorism, different in many ways from anything that had occurred previously.

The scale of the attack

In total, more than 3,000 people died, making this by far the worst single terrorist attack in history. Although it was directed at the USA, citizens of around sixty countries perished, so the attack also affected an unprecedented range of nationalities.

It confirmed a trend in global terrorism: while the number of incidents has decreased since the 1980s, the average number killed in each attack has risen. Since 1983, there have been seven attacks resulting in the deaths of a hundred or more people. This may reflect the changing nature of terrorism. The post-1968 nationalist or ideological terrorists were at least partly concerned not to lose popular support by causing indiscriminate bloodshed. The post-1980 religious terrorists believe they are carrying out God's will and care far less about public opinion. The shock factor – an essential aspect of all terrorism – is also harder to achieve in today's more violent times, and has led to an escalation in scale.

The nature of the attack

In previous aeroplane hijackings, terrorists would *threaten* to kill the hostages if their demands were not met. Sometimes hostages died during failed rescue attempts, but that was never the original object. On 11 September, the terrorists' aim was simply to kill as many people as possible. They deliberately hijacked planes on long-distance flights from Boston to the west coast, knowing they would be full of fuel. They intended the fuel tanks to explode on impact and start fires that would engulf the buildings. They also timed the attacks for when people were either arriving for work or already at their desks.

A member of the Islamic militant group HAMAS holds a hand grenade and wears an explosive belt around his waist in symbolic identification with suicide bombers, during a HAMAS rally in Gaza in October 2000.

The attack proved that terrorists do not require weapons of mass destruction – chemical, biological or nuclear – to inflict massive casualty rates. Their only weapons were the small knives or box-cutters they used to take control of the planes. The terrorists realized that a pilot – knowing he would die anyway – would not deliberately fly his plane into a building full of people, so each of the four hijack teams included trained pilots.

One of the most shocking aspects of the 11 September attacks was the fact that so many of the terrorists were willing to sacrifice their own lives. Suicide has been an established feature of terrorism for many years. Ten members of the IRA starved themselves to death in the 1980s, and five members of the German Baader-Meinhof gang also killed themselves. Since the 1990s, there have been many incidents involving suicide bombers – especially members of Islamic terrorist groups – detonating themselves in crowded places. According to the new fundamentalist version of Islam, the martyr (one who dies for his beliefs) is guaranteed a place in heaven.

It emerged that the 11 September terrorists had been living in the USA for months, leading apparently normal lives. It is possible that not all nineteen terrorists knew they were going to die (only six suicide notes have been found). Nevertheless, it is clear that al Qaida, with their connections throughout the Arab world, are able to recruit sizeable numbers of fanatical terrorists for suicide missions in remote places.

Mohamed Atta

Abdulaziz Alomari

**2001 Blue Nissan Altima
Massachusetts Registration 3335VI**

VIEWPOINTS

'... be happy with a happy heart, be confident because you are doing a job that religion accepts and loves. And then there will be a day that you will spend with beautiful angels in paradise. Oh young Man, keep a smiling face. You are on your way to everlasting paradise.'
A translation of part of a note written by Mohammed Atta, one of the terrorists, on the evening before the mission:

'Attacking innocent people is not courageous; it is stupid and will be punished on the day of judgment. It's not courageous to attack innocent children, women, and civilians. It is courageous to protect freedom; it is courageous to defend oneself and not to attack.'
Sheikh Mohammed Sayyed al-Tantawi of Al-Azhar mosque and university, Cairo, Egypt, 14 September 2001.

Photos of September 11 hijacking suspects Mohammed Atta (left) and Abdul Aziz Al-Omari (right), released by the FBI in Portland, Maine, on 4 October 2001. The men were said to be driving the car shown, a blue Nissan, while in the Portland area the day before the hijackings.

weblinks
For more information about
the war on terrorism go to
www.waylinks.co.uk/
21debatesterrorism

The war on terrorism

The 11 September attacks shocked the world
because no one had ever anticipated that anyone –
even terrorists – could be so callous as to use planes
carrying innocent civilians as missiles to attack
buildings full of equally innocent people. In the
weeks following the tragedy, as America and other
countries mourned their dead, the US government
planned its response.

Two days after the attacks, President George W.
Bush announced that America would lead the
world in a war on terrorism. This new war would
involve the use of military force against al Qaida
and other terrorist networks. But it would also
include less visible action – against terrorist
finances, build-up of weapons, and organized crime
(the drugs trade is a major source of terrorist
funding). Economic, diplomatic and military
pressure would be placed on countries that funded
and supported terrorism.

Operation Enduring Freedom

By the end of September 2001, Osama bin Laden
and his al Qaida network had been linked to the
attacks. About forty nations joined a broad
coalition, some offering moral support, others
offering military facilities and intelligence, and full
military assistance. The first stage in the war on
terror was named Operation Enduring Freedom.
Its targets were Afghanistan's regime, the Taliban,
who had refused to hand over Osama bin Laden,
and al Qaida's terrorist camps in eastern
Afghanistan. Military strikes were launched
on 7 October.

Within two months, the Taliban was overthrown
by a combination of American and British
bombing, and US-backed ground attacks by the
Afghan opposition forces known as the Northern

FACT

Osama bin Laden
released several video
tapes towards the
close of 2001 to
reassure his supporters
that he was still alive.
In one, released in
December, he came
closest to admitting his
involvement in the 11
September attacks, by
talking in detail about
the operation, and
claiming he had
underestimated the
damage that would be
inflicted on the World
Trade Center. A further
tape was released in
April 2002, but there is
no certainty as to
when it was recorded.

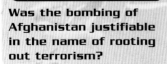

Was the bombing of
Afghanistan justifiable
in the name of rooting
out terrorism?

Fighters of the Afghan opposition Northern Alliance celebrate the withdrawal of the Taliban from Kabul, November 2001.

VIEWPOINTS

'Every nation should know that for America the war on terror is not just a policy, it's a pledge. I will not relent in this struggle for the freedom and security of my country and the civilized world.'
President George W. Bush, March 2002, during a speech at a White House memorial ceremony for the victims of 11 September

'... the United States is not "at war" in any recognisable sense of the word – certainly not a war that can be "won". It is confronted with a hideous international crime, whose perpetrators must if possible be identified, isolated, and destroyed, but in such a way that does not breed even greater hatred of the United States and even more martyrs willing to lay down their lives in the struggle against the Great Satan.'
Sir Michael Howard, former Regius Professor of Modern History at Oxford University, quoted in The Times, 14 September 2001

Alliance. Once the Taliban leadership had fled from their last stronghold in Kandahar in the south, the allied military effort focused on the mountain caves of eastern Afghanistan, where they believed bin Laden and the al Qaida leaders were hiding. Bin Laden eluded capture, but many al Qaida fighters were killed or taken prisoner.

As operations in Afghanistan drew to a close, the US began broadening its war against terrorism by providing military assistance to other countries struggling against terrorist groups, some of which had links to the al Qaida network. These included Georgia, Kyragyzstan, Uzbekistan, and the Philippines. Other countries suspected of having al Qaida cells included Indonesia, Yemen, Sudan and Somalia. There are also known or suspected al Qaida cells operating in Western European cities such as London, Hamburg, Milan and Madrid. These are important centres for recruitment, fundraising and planning operations.

TERRORISM IN THE TWENTY-FIRST CENTURY

Can it ever be eradicated?

Terrorism has changed a great deal since the 1960s. The rise of Islamic fundamentalism, the end of the Cold War, the global banking network, and the telecommunications revolution, have all played their part in changing the motives and methods of international terrorism. With the launch of the war on terrorism, it is likely to change again, adapting itself to a more hostile environment.

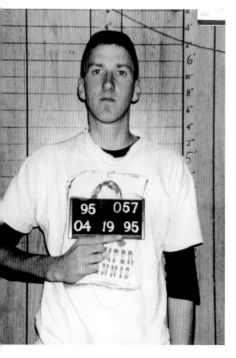

Timothy McVeigh, shown here under arrest in April 1995 and later convicted of the Oklahoma City bombing in which 168 people died. He was executed by lethal injection on 11 June 2001.

The new threat

Until the 1980s, the major players in international politics were nation-states. The security systems of the USA and its allies were set up to guard against military strikes by other countries, especially the Soviet Union or China. Terrorism was not seen as a significant threat to internal security, and terrorists were viewed more as pawns in the global chess game between the superpowers.

During the 1990s, there were signs that terrorist groups were outgrowing this lowly status, as more ambitious attacks were launched against Western interests around the world. But it was not until 11 September 2001 that the world finally woke up to the new threat.

The new threat comes not from nation-states, but from social, ethnic or religious groups living within

Oklahoma City's Alfred P. Murrah Federal Building showing the devastating effect of the truck bomb that ripped the structure apart on 19 April 1995.

those states who feel their interests have been ignored. This is particularly true of Islamic fundamentalists in Arab states, but there are other examples. For instance, Timothy McVeigh, who was responsible for a truck bomb that killed 168 people in Oklahoma City in 1995, was a white, lower middle-class, rural American. His action might be seen as an extreme reflection of the anger of a social class who feel sidelined in the rush towards modernization. Similarly, the establishment of the Aum Shinrikyo sect in Japan can be perceived as a reaction to that country's abandonment of traditional values in favour of Western culture.

By contrast, nation-states no longer pose as much of a threat to world security. Apart from certain 'rogue states', like Iraq and North Korea, most countries – or at least their governments – are becoming partners in a unified world system that embraces modernization and globalization. This includes even former enemies of the West, such as China and Russia.

FACT

The Japanese religious movement Aum Shinrikyo was established in 1987. As well as the 1995 sarin gas attack it carried out in Tokyo, the sect was involved in kidnapping and murder. However, in January 2000 the group dissociated itself from its original founder, established a new code of conduct which prohibited its 2,000 members from breaking the law, and renamed itself 'Aleph'.

weblinks

For more information about Aum Shinrikyo go to www.waylinks.co.uk/ 21debatesterrorism

VIEWPOINT

'The fundamental rule guiding the organization of the Free Militia is generalized principles and planning but decentralized tactics and action... Thus, there must be allegiance to a higher command. But specific tactics should be left up to the individual elements... Furthermore, all training and combat actions should be up to the smaller elements, again so that isolation or decapitation does not render the smaller units inept.'
An extreme right-wing American terrorist organization explains the need for a flexible structure: 'Field Manual Section 1: Principles Justifying the Arming and Organizing of A Militia'. The Free Militia. Wisconsin. USA

Asymmetric warfare

The West must now adapt its foreign policy, its armed forces and security systems to confront an enemy that occupies no identifiable territory, possesses no towns or cities, but is hidden and dispersed in many locations, always able to attack with the advantage of surprise. This new kind of confrontation, between nations and terrorist groups, is known as 'asymmetric warfare' because it is between a large force and a weak force. Systems developed during the Cold War, such as National Missile Defence – a space-based defensive shield against ballistic missile attack – are of limited use in asymmetric warfare. They will not protect the West from future terrorist attacks, whether they come in the form of bombs, hijackings, or germ warfare.

The 11 September attacks illustrated, for the first time, some key characteristics of terrorism in the twenty-first century. These include hitting the enemy at its strategic centres (which include government and military targets) and its symbolic centres. The World Trade Center symbolizes American economic power and US-led globalization. The Pentagon is the symbol of American military power, and it can be assumed that the fourth plane was heading for one of its centres of political power – either the White House or

Catholic youths in Ireland prepare makeshift petrol bombs to use against their Loyalist adversaries. Terrorists are adept at causing maximum impact with meagre resources.

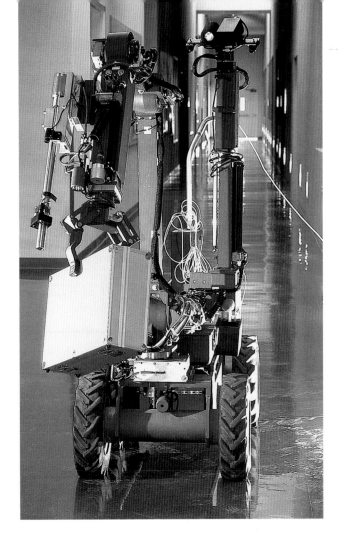

Counter-terrorist agencies are turning increasingly to new technology, such as this bomb disposal robot, Wolverine.

Congress. By contrast, most terrorist organizations are deliberately structured so they have no identifiable centres at which a country can strike back.

Aware of how highly life is valued in Western society, the 11 September terrorists aimed to kill as many people as possible. The attacks can also be seen partly as propaganda for the terrorists' comrades and supporters back home. The message they wished to convey was clear: the USA, despite its great military power, can be successfully attacked by a combination of low-tech tools, ingenuity and human resolve.

Terrorists in the twenty-first century will exploit the weaknesses of Western democracies – such as their visibility, their lack of secrecy, their need to maintain popular support, and their slowness to react to altered circumstances. Terrorists, by contrast, can operate in secret, they have fewer qualms about using violence, they can move quickly and make use of surprise.

In these new conditions of asymmetric warfare, Western nations need to find ways of overcoming or minimizing the capabilities of the terrorists.

FACT

Most Western countries are now spending far more on security against terrorism. For example, between 1996 and 2001, US federal spending to combat terrorism rose by more than 50 per cent to approximately $10 billion. This included spending on intelligence, border security, and covert operations.

They must identify the terrorists' points of vulnerability and exploit them with equal ruthlessness and cunning.

After 11 September 2001, there was a stronger collective will among nation-states to confront terrorism together. This led to some surprising realignments in global politics, with both China and Russia allying themselves with the USA against the new threat.

There was also an acceptance among some nations that serious measures – including military action – were sometimes appropriate in the altered circumstances. The Taliban of Afghanistan in 2001 were the first in the firing line. Since then, however, a split has emerged between the world's leading powers over the next stage in the war on terrorism. France, Russia and China all opposed the American and British attack on Iraq in 2003.

A counter-attack against terrorism is also being launched in the world of finance. The global banking system is changing its methods of operation to make it harder for terrorists to transfer their funds between bank accounts; and the flow of capital may be restricted. This will affect legitimate trade as well, but governments accept that sacrifices will need to be made. Similarly, the intelligence services of countries around the world are pooling their knowledge and gradually discovering links between terrorism and organized crime.

In addition, governments are reorganizing their defences. Because terrorists can strike at the heart of towns and cities, a much greater emphasis will be placed on civil defence. Future governments may spend as much on protecting their citizens as they do on their armed forces.

weblinks

For more information about counter-terrorist activity go to www.waylinks.co.uk/ 21debatesterrorism

Weapons of mass destruction

One particularly alarming aspect of the new threat is the possibility that terrorist groups might get hold of weapons of mass destruction (WMD). These fall into three categories: nuclear, biological and chemical.

Nuclear weapons work by a process known as nuclear fission, in which the nucleus of an atom is split into smaller nuclei, releasing a substantial amount of energy. When the nuclei of certain materials, such as uranium-235, undergo this process in a chain reaction, the energy released can flatten a city.

A biological weapon is a missile, bomb or other device used to deliver deadly micro-organisms. They can even be delivered into a community by animals, especially rodents or insects.

Rather than full-scale nuclear explosions like these, terrorists are more likely to develop radiological bombs, which mainly cause casualties through radioactive contamination.

A chemical weapon delivers and spreads toxic substances to damage or kill humans, animals or plantlife. These include poisonous gases like chlorine gas and mustard gas, which were used in the First World War.

Biological and chemical weapons have been produced or obtained by terrorist groups in the past. In 1995, the Aum Shinrikyo cult released an odourless but lethal nerve gas known as sarin on the Tokyo underground, killing twelve people and injuring over 5,000. Other agents used in terrorist attacks have included tear gas, cyanide, acid, insecticides, and anthrax.

There have been several chemical and biological attacks in recent years, most of them in the USA. However, there are significant technical hurdles that terrorists will have to overcome if they are to achieve mass casualty rates, such as finding effective modes of delivery. The most likely methods are by introducing a toxic agent into foods or drinks, or into a city's water supply, or by deliberately infecting people with a contagious disease.

An anthrax-laced letter sent to the editor of the New York Post *on 23 October 2001. The FBI offered a $2 million dollar reward to anyone who provided information leading to the arrest and conviction of the person responsible for these letters. The person has yet to be found.*

Thankfully, nuclear weapons are very difficult to produce. The specific types of uranium or plutonium required are not naturally occurring; they need to be bought or stolen. Furthermore, the actual building of a nuclear bomb requires a team of scientists with very specialized skills. However, a crude type of nuclear weapon, known as a radiological bomb, could be more easily developed.

A barrel of phosphorus trichloride – used in the production of sarin – is confiscated from the Aum Shinrikyo sect in Japan. Though deadly, sarin is relatively simple to produce.

The chief threats from WMD come from technologically sophisticated terrorists, or well-funded groups like al Qaida. Osama bin Laden has told his followers it is their 'religious duty' to obtain WMD, and there is evidence from documents and laboratory equipment captured from al Qaida bases in Afghanistan that they were attempting to develop them. At one training camp, thirty boxes were discovered containing phials labelled 'Sarin'.

Terrorism in the future

So long as there remain groups of people in society who feel excluded from its benefits, whose desires or interests are ignored, or who are simply oppressed, and so long as those people have access to arms, there will always be terrorism. The terrorists of today are more sophisticated, more ruthless, and more deadly than ever before. On the positive side, the world finally seems to have woken up to the threat they pose, and countries are now working together to confront the international menace of terrorism.

DEBATE

Will terrorism, like war and poverty, always be with us – or can we be rid of it?

Pembroke Branch Tel. 6689575

GLOSSARY

amnesty a general pardon, especially for people who have committed political crimes.

anarchist someone who rejects the need for a government, and supports its abolition.

arsenal a stockpile of weapons and armaments.

asymmetric warfare warfare conducted between powers of unequal strength, e.g. a nation and a group.

Bolsheviks a radical group within the Russian Socialist party that took power in the Russian Revolution of 1917.

capitalism an economic system characterized by a free competitive market and based on private ownership of the means of production.

cell a small group within an organization.

chain reaction a series of events, each of which causes the next one.

civil liberties basic rights guaranteed to citizens by law, such as freedom of speech.

colonial powers European powers, including Britain, France, Belgium, Germany, Spain and Portugal, which ruled over countries in other parts of the world in the nineteenth and twentieth centuries.

communism a system, or the belief in a system, in which control of wealth and property resides with the state and is shared equally by the people.

counter-revolutionary opposed to revolution.

covert action secret action

extradition the handing over by a government of an individual accused of committing a crime in a different country, for trial and punishment in the country where the crime was committed.

extremism extreme or radical beliefs.

faction a group existing within a larger group that holds views not always in agreement with the larger group.

fanaticism an extreme and often irrational belief.

fascism a nationalistic, often racist, ideology that favours strong leadership and does not tolerate dissent.

fatwah a formal religious ruling issued by an Islamic leader.

fundamentalism a usually religious movement or attitude emphasizing the strict following of a set of basic principles.

guerilla a member of an unofficial military force, usually with some political objective such as the overthrow of a government.

heretic somebody who holds beliefs that contradict official or established religious views within a country or culture.

humanitarian committed to improving the lives of other people.

ideology a system of beliefs that forms the basis of a social, economic or political philosophy or programme.

infrastructure the public systems, services and facilities of a country that are necessary for it to function, such as roads, railways, power and water supplies, and telecommunications.

launder (used in the financial sense) to pass illegally acquired money through a legitimate business or bank account in order to disguise its illegal origins.

left-wing (of political beliefs) supporting liberal, socialist or communist political and social change or reform.

liberal democratic (of a political system)

having free elections, several political parties, and a government that is checked and balanced by laws and judges.

mediator somebody who works with both sides in a dispute in order to help them reach an agreement.

militant extremely active in support of a cause, often to an extent that causes conflict with other people or institutions.

multiculturalism the process of, or belief in, the integration of people of different countries, ethnic groups and religions into all areas of society.

nation-state an independent state that is recognized by other states and interacts with them.

nationalist supportive of the right of one's people to exist as a nation, or belief in the status of one's nation above all others.

Nazi Germany Germany between 1933 and 1945 when it was ruled by the National Socialist (Nazi) Party under Adolf Hitler.

neo-Nazi a member of a modern-day group who believe in the supremacy of a white race, and engage in attacks on non-white people.

organized crime crime committed by large and powerful networks of criminals, including drug trafficking, gambling and prostitution.

Ottoman Empire a Turkish empire established in the late thirteenth century in Asia Minor, eventually extending through the Middle East and into parts of North Africa, which came to an end in 1922.

patriotic pride in one's country.

proxy war a war between two powers that is fought by others, e.g. smaller countries, guerilla forces or terrorist groups.

psychosis psychiatric disorder, such as schizophrenia, that is marked by delusions, incoherence, and distorted perceptions of reality.

radical supportive of extreme political, economic or social change.

relief worker someone who helps to bring and distribute aid to suffering people, usually following a natural or man-made disaster.

repressive exerting strict control over the freedom of others.

right-wing (of political beliefs) wishing to preserve traditional ways of life, and unwilling or slow to accept change or new ideas.

sect a small, close-knit religious group.

self-determination the right of a people to determine its own form of government without interference from outside.

separatist a person or group who is in favour of breaking away from a larger group, organization or country.

socialist relating to, or belief in, a political system in which wealth is shared equally between people, and the main industries and trade are controlled by the government.

Sunni Muslim follower of the largest branch of Islam.

totalitarian relating to a centralized government system in which a single party controls all political, economic, social and cultural life.

white-supremacist relating to, or belief in, the supremacy of white Anglo-Saxon people over all other races or ethnic groups.

TERRORIST GROUPS

ANC	African National Congress (South Africa)
ELN	National Liberation Army (Colombia)
ETA	Euzkadi to Askatasuna – Basque Fatherland and Liberty (Spain)
FLN	Fronte de Liberation Nationale (Algeria)
FLQ	Fronte Liberation Quebec (Canada)
IRA	Irish Republican Army (Ireland)
JRA	Japanese Red Army (Japan)
LTTE	Liberation Tigers of Tamil Eelam (Sri Lanka)
PKK	Kurdish Worker's Party (Turkey)
PLO	Palestine Liberation Organization (Israel)
RAF	Red Army Faction (West Germany)
SL	Sendero Luminoso (Shining Path)

BOOKS TO READ

Why are People Terrorists?
Alex Woolf
(Hodder Wayland, 2003)

Troubled World: The Arab-Israeli Conflict
Ivan Minnis
(Heinemann Library, 2001)

Lives in Crisis: Conflict in Northern Ireland
R. G. Grant
(Hodder Wayland, 2001)

Troubled World: The Troubles in Northern Ireland
Ivan Minnis
(Heinemann Library, 2002)

Ideas of the Modern World: Communism
Nigel Richie
(Hodder Wayland, 2000)

What's At Issue: War and Conflict
Sean Connolly
(Heinemann Library, 2002)

SOURCES

International Terrorism
Charles W. Kegley (ed.)
(St Martin's Press, 1990)

How Did This Happen? Terrorism and the New War
James Hoge and Gideon Rose (eds.)
(Public Affairs, 2001)

The New Face of Terrorism: Threats from Weapons of Mass Destruction
Nadine Gurr and Benjamin Cole
(Tauris, 2000)

The Culture of Terrorism
Noam Chomsky
(Pluto Press, 1988)

The New Terrorism
Walter Laqueur
(Phoenix Press, 2001)

One Day in September
Simon Reeve
(Faber and Faber, 2001)

Terrorism Today
Christopher C. Harmon
(Cass, 2000)

Websites

For additional topics that are relevant to this book go to
www.waylinks.co.uk/21debatesterrorism

INDEX

Numbers in **bold** refer to illustrations.